MW01098738

The Luskville Reductions

The Luskville Reductions
Monty Reid

Brick Books

Library and Archives Canada Cataloguing in Publication

Reid, Monty, 1952-
    The Luskville reductions / Monty Reid.

Poems.
ISBN 978-1-894078-65-8

    1. Luskville (Pontiac, Québec)—Poetry.   I. Title.

PS8585.E603L88 2008   C811'.54   C2008-900475-2

We acknowledge the support of the Canada Council for the
Arts, the Government of Canada through the Book Publishing
Industry Development Program (BPIDP), and the Ontario Arts
Council for their support of our publishing program.

    Canada

The photograph on the cover is "Erosions in Granite" by
Adrian R. Searle, October 2004.

The author's photograph is by John MacDonald.

The book is set in Minion Pro and Rotis Sans.

Design and layout by Alan Siu.

Printed and bound by Sunville Printco Inc.

Brick Books
431 Boler Road, Box 20081
London, Ontario N6K 4G6

www.brickbooks.ca

For Sarah Hill

Nothing can be reduced to anything else.

– Bruno Latour

My substance was not hid from thee, when I was made in secret, and curiously wrought in the lowest parts of the earth.
– Psalm 139: 15, 16

Luskville is a phantom settlement on the Ottawa River in western Quebec. I lived there for five years, until my partner, nursing a suite of dissatisfactions, returned to Alberta in 1994. Before she left, she planted a dozen varieties of daylilies.

The problem with daylilies
is the usual contemporary twaddle: how is it
we know anything
                    now that you're gone.

What do you mean
                    now that you're gone?

What do you mean
                    daylilies?

❖

Green strands of algae in the frog pond
connective tissue

something coming into this world
instead of

well, instead of
the body
at the end of my arms.

What is it you want to know?

Slick frogs
stick their noses out of the water
as if they were watching for something.

We are all still here.

And that's the point isn't it?
To continue.

Not just to remember
but to remain.

Woof of bullfrogs that first hot night
woof of data in the archives.

Oh they sing
through the hot air

for the uncatalogued
loves. For whatever

one can say about them.
Take the air

the hood of air over us
take it off.

The rain is finished

but the way rain beads on the dented fenders
of what has been loved

isn't.

The rain is finished

but the sheen of rain still on the concrete
isn't.

Rags of light
pegged behind the thunderclouds.

The rain is finished
but there is always something

in the lid of the body
that resists

and something with bigger holes in it
than the holes in rain.

What is nature, anyway?
asked my friend over lunch

as if it had been inadequately theorized
or perhaps because we hadn't seen each other in years

and he thought
maybe I'd have some idea by now

but I didn't have any kind of answer
other than to pick up my fork

and cut into the lamb with figs and pomegranate
which he'd recommended.

So my theory is nature is never an answer
but a question

just not the question
I needed to ask at the time.

Like a fork.
Like the hand around it.

Like the other hand too.

❖

Yes the faculty of language
is the condition a priori *de tout genre de discours*

but being alive in the world
is the condition a priori *de toute faculté de langage.*

Consider: hinged beetles
            yes, hinged beetles

            eat the world.

The animals arrived
that year
to help us

first the large golden dog, with tags,
showed up on our doorstep and calmly sat down to wait

and then the pure white pigeon, banded,
that sheltered under our eaves after the big storm
and stayed for a week

and the young rabbit, tame,
that sat on the balcony in December
and ate the bottom half of the cedars

and the squirrels and the bullfrogs
and the stilted herons
they all made their appearance

and we sent them
wild or just lost
on their way.

How long did it take us
to discover

we were sliding into the river?

Tilt of dirt in the garden

or the morning we awoke
rolled into a corner
of the room

and couldn't remember
anything except
some vigorous love-making

or the doors
that no longer shut properly

but do shut.

The upgraded surfaces
yes

the cold surfaces
yes

the marble the granite the smoked glass
surfaces yes

the corian the stainless the bemused
surfaces.

The dust assembles.

It has found us
because it was looking for us.

Slowly

entering you
I unproduce myself

undo
the raw material

easily

as your small
black dress

removed

some time ago.

The nipple
rises
to the tongue

how often?

we were together 32 years
let's say we had sex on average two times a week
allowing for absences or sick leave
or the above average holidays
and that hi-rate first year

that would be 32 times 52 times 2
equals 3328

and the nipple
still rises
to the tongue

times 2.

Oh my sticky
baby

can you remember
being taken up

as one would take up
a life

a fiddle playing
repetitively

and someone
frailing a banjo

keep that skillet good and greasy
all the time, time, time.

Too early
or too late

or we were not
there at all

that's why you practice
isn't it

so when that song comes around
you can play it.

❖

Yes
I still have the mandolin.

I can play it
modestly.

My little finger
wears a hole

right through the finish
and down into the soft wood.

Every song I learn
works its way through

whatever
makes the song possible.

Yes, it looks bad
that worn down surface

but down there
where the sound is made

it still sounds ok.

❖

Spackle
of cherts and quartzite

a granite wall
for a backyard.

Perhaps they outlive us.

Evidence of heat
outlives the heat.

If you don't have flesh
then not having flesh

will have to do.

I wish I could say
that we unravelled
quietly

but

there's the banjo.

Nails pop in the siding

old friends show up
from the same exactitudes

with that
same look of surprise.

A rusty tear will begin
around each one of them

and seep down
the flaking white paint.

The repair of the world
is endless.

Get the hammer.
Pound them back down.

Broke my watch

was it yesterday?

Smacked the glass
hard on a corner of cinder block

when I was trying to jack up
the porch

like I promised.
Before you got back.

Its delicate hands
quivered and of course
there was sand all over it.

It couldn't remember
anything.

At the strip north of the river
hi-octane dragsters
burn up the track.

I know
you hated that snarl
that combustion

but I got used to it.

How what remains
after the seconds are peeled away

two black strips,
perfectly spaced,

the smell of burnt rubber.

The bright orange and yellow
windsock
you bought on a trip to PEI

fills up with wind

no matter where
the wind comes from

it points the other direction.

Lying somewhere
between us

the remote
that little box
of signals and intentions

is always black
why is that?

How many channels in a universe?
How much distance does it take

to chew the wavelengths?
Ghost flutter.

Hands that arrive
if at all

from somewhere not that well defined.

Ok
you hold it.

❖

The thistles
know they aren't wanted

and it makes them exuberant.

They want you to touch them.

Lux of mid-summer
everything lamped and on
surplus and everywhere.

Which heaven
do you think we can't take?

On the periphery
nothing changes

wrecks of clouds
sink on the south horizon all day

although a wind
a hot late July wind
dredges the shallow bay
where the heron stalked

beautiful air at the margins of things

feathers of edges, hulls scuttled, the dust-light
of horizons

a bird always
between it.

The light
which is just a filament

that resists
is on late

and the moths
always the same

soft-hinged moths
accumulate on the screen.

Their antennae
bend up into the technologies

signals of disaster enrich them
they know the talks have failed

the light that burned so late
is going out

and the visible
has become just another invention.

They close their wings.
This is as close

as they can get.

A priori
the August heat loves only itself.

It has been admiring itself
in the upstairs bedroom
all afternoon.

But now you have opened
all the windows
to try to get the air moving

and stripped down to your underwear
and stood for a moment
in front of the fan.

It swivels on its long neck
away from you

then swivels back.

Silver water
black water

lead and aluminum
running nickel

and platinum tossed
to the moonlight.

One small boat

someone has painted *weltgeist*
on its side

bumps against the dock
all night.

Your hands feel like stepping into a sauna
was what you said.

Look at them - scars, callouses
a small lump from holding a pen the same way for years

fingertips hard as the tense strings, as
the discontinued music

all the nails chipped at the corners
where somebody tried to pry them open
and couldn't

two stubborn thumbs
because who could be happy opposing one thing at a time

and on their backs
the big dialectical veins fork giving you the choice:

total knowability of the body
or, a thumb

and then there's all that proletarian hair that thrives, I guess
in heat and humidity.

And you thought of them as a sauna.
It may have been the nicest thing you said to me.

I keep looking at them, surprised
at their past.

A bit jealous.

Tv glow
from the other room.

It's always the light
from this world

that follows you around.

They say that if you live together
long enough

you and your television
begin to resemble one another.

It's ok. Before the end
all images begin to look alike.

Paradise
wiggles out of its clasps

et voilà
it's just

everything you've
already seen.

You walk into the room
and your hair
comes along behind

a little reluctantly
I think

you've cut it
and dyed it red
and it still smells of the salon.

I don't think it's completely
used to you
yet

when you turn to go
it stays for a moment

then it goes too.

❖

Flakes and edges
a load of crushed shale for the driveway

mud from the Champlain Sea
no light in it.

Flakes and edges
and a long-handled
shovel.

I shouldn't have

but yesterday I stacked
9 cords of dry hardwood

and split an armful
of kindling.

Oh I'm stiff and sore
and have all the vague aches
of the unready

and the fire
is once again

perfectly shaped
where you built it.

At night the single red light
out in the main channel
of the Ottawa

flashes
automatically

flight path of a dream
that circles and circles

and can't survive
the landing.

We left it too late

and the water's freezing
when we bring the dock in.

It makes the skin burn
once you're out of it.

Treated planks in their dry racks
rustproof frame up by the hedge of white cedars

where it catches thousands of oak leaves
that have to let go, one

fire at a time.

❖

When I finally
gathered up the garden hose
late September

an image of its soul
remained in loops on the sidewalk.

Like all souls
it was made out of a speckle
of dust and dead bugs.

I rolled the so-called
unkinkable hose
around its plastic spindle.

A last trickle of summer water
spilled out

at both ends.

Dark house
fridge hum, fan hum

red lights everywhere

tv, smoke detector, microwave
computer, clock, etc

even the tiny nightlight
that glows by your bed

that say
we're not on

but we're ready.

Grey morning

gridded with
bands of apricot

over the distant
office blocks
of Kanata.

My neighbour
is up early

for a long weekend.

He's lit his pipe
and watches the sunrise

thinking
that no one
is watching him

and that the second-hand
smoke of paradise

runs deep in the river's
marrow

right past us.

❖

In the weft of fog
nothing

is distinguishable
from the fog.

It descends, the
pure fur, the pure

production of a space
occupied only by itself

flesh still attached.

❖

The constellations
arrange themselves
over the black river

with their latin names
and higher mathematics
of the sleepless

to consider.

If they can do it
so can you.

Tonight a breeze from upriver
rejigs the top branches
of the big oak

green acorns fall on the roof
decisively

then bounce once or twice
with their second thoughts.

Clusters of leaves
whish into the longitudes

and in the morning
diagrams of dead branches
scratched on the lawn.

I am awake
again

a slight fragrance in the room
or the memory of a slight fragrance

like the lotion I rubbed into your shoulders
and the hard little scar low on your back
where you had the mole removed

dead skin you said

but at night it would shine a little
anyway.

How far away
is it, again?

Rub the stars
and the glow still finds us

even though the source is vanishing
at incomprehensible speed.

Tonight
the ghosts are wearing
your shoes

the shoes you bought
specifically
to go dancing in.

This time
they'll keep your shoes

but change
their feet.

One hard morning
red blows out of the trees

too fast and loose for anything
with one good leg to keep up to

and the fall foliage tours
are off

just like that.

In the rescheduled afternoon
sunlight the leaves gather

in drifts along Chemin
de la Montagne

and agree they never wanted
celebrity status anyway.

It's what the trees say too
now that they're standing

there, arm in arm
naked.

Once, for your birthday
which I never forgot

I made a card of pixie cups and sleeping mosses
from the shaded ridge above our house

and once, for our anniversary
with its flexible date

I gave you a bouquet of spray-painted tubing that said
my love is like a red, red hose.

Now I am making a card
for all occasions

out of your sheer underwear
with the exact red hearts

that are sometimes in us
and sometimes

precisely not.

Oh the slag
of memory

I don't want it.

The skanks of late-night
meditations

you keep them.

The vanilla candles, the diaries
all the data

it's yours.

But the sweet air
that entered you

and came back to the space
of the world much reduced

but remixed and yes
sometimes looking for me

it's still out there
and no one's.

All the fragments, splinters, rogue signals
the heart claims to receive

inadvertently

its ghost lineage

> years full of information
> and what did I ever know?

parsimonious elements
sift in the atmospheres

salts in the blood
phantom languages

> a body is not separate
> I am not asking what disappeared
> I'm asking what was here

the stumps, the relict populations
the extra bones

all the evidence

is useless
if it loves you.

❖

November, so

the last box of tomatoes
sits in the kitchen
green with envy.

They will soften
and turn red all at once

too many to eat.

They are a little embarrassed
by their sense
of timing

but this is the world
they were given.

One hunger is never enough
for it.

Getting up to pee
middle of the night
and pausing at the south window

hello
red Mars
gleaming on its wires

as close as it will ever be
in our lifetime.

Hello it says
what wires?

In every
thing

is room
for another

all the hard work

that goes into
one more kiss

the lips the lips the lips

that go
into all the hard work.

Moon wallow

a mist shivers
out of the river.

No, it isn't absence
nothing

is this version
of absence.

The long
stalks of light

clutch at the shimmer
then let it go.

❖

Where I am
is a space in my body

not the raw material for anything
else.

The body is never lost.
So is never saved.

No matter where it detaches
the dead

and the living.
Still

where I am remains faithful
to the physical

twist, the enter of wavelengths
between one line

and another
uncertain of the nature of what they love

ruined motion of all those particles

rattling around in
the undiminished space

of a thing
you end up

and have to live in.

❖

Don't expect the truth
from any of the things you took.

I'm not the first to remark that they lie
even when they don't need to.

Just as I won't trust anything
you left behind.

I found the book, Elizabeth Bishop's
complete poems

I thought was lost.
No, to be honest
I thought you had taken it.

As for the unfinished songs
I left on your computer

delete them

let them go into the sub-drives
of memory

or finish them and claim them as
yours.

Then they will be.

The chimes, splinters
of obsidian strung with fishing line

bought at a ferry dock so
many years ago and hung above

the windy deck beside the river
turn the wind
in their fingers of old glass.

Where were we going?
Down there beside the water.

I can't remember.

After the storm broke them
we found the pieces
and glued them back together

except for all the bits
that didn't fit anywhere.

I have learned
to arrange my life

so I don't have to cross
the Champlain Bridge at
rush hour.

Everything else is fine.

In the early evening
old men lean
over the metal rails.

Perhaps
they are praying

the way their hands
extend in front of them.

They eat
whatever they catch.

❖

The light
we can measure

all its sparks and burning
tissue

no matter how old

countable lumens
flare
of your thighs
etc

but measuring it
is not living in it.

Close your eyes.
The estimates of dark

are just that

whatever it takes
to keep them closed.

I have become
similar to what
can be remembered.

It was my greatest fear.

What has become
of the room of desire

is just the desire for
a room.

Grey morning
fogs the edges off.

The river
has been running
over everything

just the same.

To become the other

is always to become
the same

a mob of smooth pebbles
at the river edge

never forget.

The river can't be naked
enough

to come into this room.

Only a small part of yourself
belongs

to yourself here.

Not the naked part.

Every morning

bones click
into place

with less precision.

The knee, the wrist
long gravities
of vertebrae.

Stiff oils
of October weather
gathering behind the clouds

less and less
articulate.

Still, they fit.

They measure
and they fit.

The rake is there
to lean upon

like the closely-related
species, the shovel
and the hoe.

It has a top
and a bottom
a backwards and forwards

a place for hands
and a causal relationship
with leaves

which is why
I have come to avoid
the rake

which is leaning against
the south rail
of the deck

with its teeth

right where you left it.

Upriver
shotguns

and in the pre-dawn
fog, a black barge

draped with
camouflage

drifts silently
in the shallows

like something
out of *La Morte d'Arthur*

but it's just hunting season.

The last geese
whistle through the air

among the pellets
in this expanding universe

which can't go backwards
any more.

On the night table beside the bed
you have abandoned
temporarily

stand the brown bottles
of alternative
cures.

The ingredients
are a mystery
but the handwritten labels
all say take 5 drops

so I do
and feel the improvement
right away.

My breath
smells like lavender
or the first taste of an apple.

Something in this room
could get better.

Let the fat notes
resonate. The new songs are all about you

just like the old songs were
and the black leather guitar strap

you bought so many years ago
much softened

by reaching around my
shoulders to something

that never existed there behind me
reaches around me again

for the same
incurable reasons.

The flu season
is here

with its new
off-shore varieties.

Its epidemiology
is well established.

Wherever you are
I always get it

from you.

❖

You taught me to count
so I'm counting the wooden chopsticks

we brought home from the restaurant
one, two, one, two

one.

You taught me to save
so I'm saving the fortune cookie

just one
from the last time we ate there.

About the size of your mouth
with words in it

millions.

❖

I don't have any pictures
anymore
but I'm old enough to remember

when electricity came to some houses
out in the Saskatchewan bush

how we gathered
among the hot currents to celebrate
and in addition to the sandwiches

and beer, everyone
brought a new before, a new after
and an extra 60-watt bulb.

It's not quite a myth of origins
is it

although the light adds years
to every face

even yours.

The fall rains
dream grey water.

Mud forms
and forms mud

anonymously

then you step in it.

One still morning
just before Christmas

the huts of the ice fishermen
appear

out over the deep current.

They drill a hole though the ice

anything
to be the centre of attention.

Black water takes the bait.
They have learned

patience.

A thin line of smoke
runs from

the tin chimney
straight up.

Birds winch into the sky

the heart on its pulleys

the hinges of winter

all the beautiful machines

stop.

stop.

❖

I couldn't stop

but now
I've stopped.

What is the suitable distance
between stopping
and saying
you have stopped?

Between writing
and saying you have written?

It's not the fall that kills you.

Say the falling.

Yes we spent some time
at that temple of dishes
in the sink

the forks prayed
the knives prayed
they were baptized

and reborn.

Hallelujah I say
Amen.

I'll wash
and you dry.

The horizon is always pushing the same line

though it is not itself the same line
all the time.

What is the space of distance
of one distance

what is it made of
that it comes to mind like this

and no way to explain it.

It has a spiritual, or some would say
theoretical, side, the side you can never see.

And there is the side that is oblivion

that rolls itself in the dirt from time to time
and look, it still glows.

This is the line it is always pushing:

        I am bigger than you
        I am bigger than you
        I am so much bigger than you.

Nonetheless
you are gone over it.

The one side of it.

You
are gone over it.

I was waiting for you
there, the neutral place you wanted

and a February wind appeared by mistake.

It turned again and again
caught in the raw concrete square, hemmed

in by dressed stone, by the brown perimeter cedars
lining the wrought-iron fence.

Who knows where it came from.

Sympathetic debris convinced that what is closed
against the world is also
the world

lifts up. Napkins
smudged on mouths and fingers

kiss of lipstick on a paper cup
ripped envelopes addressed to *occupant*

beautiful litter
everything

the lips have touched.

Does the weather
move to some kind of resolution?

Theoretically, no.

Mid-March, and the river ice undoes itself
the ideology of water
lifts it

slow groan in the limbs, deep
in the run

low-resolution
faults tromped into the structure

directly under your feet
although they sound as if they
were miles away

and they are.

Colour of April.
Les chutes roared

falling down the hard stairs
of the Gatineaus
overflowing the creek

and flooding the
only road in
for a week.

We got to work at home
for a couple of days
then it all subsided.

The moon, which
had been reflected
in acres of waterbound cornfields

makes do
with something less.

The claim, for instance
that there never was any reflection

and the claim
that it was working all the time.

The new roof
attracts the spring rain.

Stains
appear again on the ceiling.

This is how the dream-life of rain
gets interpreted.

The outside leaks in
and someone explains it.

Whoever has to fix
the roof again

just stops dreaming.

I think the soul
is really

just the little black off-the-shoulder dress
you wore to the office party.

In the morning there it is
on the floor.

And I think the heart
is that delicate necklace with its solitaire

that reflected
even the most ephemeral moonlight.

It's on the floor
too.

I think that the past
just has to wear

itself out
and that a kiss can be removed

and wrapped up in the tissue it came in
until it's needed again.

Some party.

Does anyone need boxes?

I've got hundreds.
And can't stand
the smell of cardboard anymore.

All that space
that was inside them
is still a space somewhere

but these boxes are empty.

I pulled them apart and calmed down
all those loose flaps
and flattened them

for the dumpster.

There is always
the available volume of the world.

There's always more boxes.

❖

Unexpected events
become the expected

until there is no unexpected
left

which is why every system
generates an outside
the system

and then the events much beyond

our selves
become possible

and therefore beautiful again.

Tape up the last cardboard box
and haul it away.

Put me inside you
again.

The best dreams
are deniable.

They deny, for instance
whoever you are.

They are the untold
the collapsed

the ones that contain
nothing.

Next best are the forgettable
and after that

the unrepeatable.

Ah, my skeptical baby
be careful what you love.

The bed is still warm.
It keeps saying

it wasn't me

not me
not ever.

A fine blue mold
with delicate struts
and fires

has appeared
on the one thing
you forgot

a partially-squeezed
lemon in the fridge.   .

To survive
it doesn't need much

but it will never
be satisfied with survival.

It wants everything.
Everything in the fridge

and then some.

❖

Freezing rain
and one single idea

is enough.

No thought is free of the world.
The molt of ice

suggests a larger animal.
Ok, maybe that's two.

Go home

now
while you still can.

❖

All the tall men
are captured.

Grey stalks of daylilies
all the varieties
you planted

reach their two arms
to the sky.

The rest of us give up
less gracefully

all by our selves

each time we surrender.

What descends
on all the things
of my lifetime

and makes them inexhaustible.

Was it just your kiss?

On the seams
of all the things

just the loneliness
of your mouth?

What enters?
What escapes?

Desolate
countable stars

shine.

Some of these poems have appeared in *The Malahat Review, The Fiddlehead, Prairie Fire, Inwords,* and *Ottawater.* Thank you to the editors.

Born in Saskatchewan, and a longtime resident of Alberta, Monty Reid moved to the small village of Luskville, Quebec in 1999. *The Luskville Reductions* is his 14th book. His previous books include *Crawlspace* (Anansi), *Flat Side* (Red Deer) and *Disappointment Island* (Chaudiere) which was short-listed for the Ottawa Book Award and won the 2007 Lampman-Scott Award. His books have also won three Stephan G. Stephansson Awards, and been nominated three times for the Governor-General's Award for Poetry. Monty Reid now lives in Ottawa and works at the Canadian Museum of Nature.